50 Homemade Healthy Desserts

By: Kelly Johnson

Table of Contents

- Avocado Chocolate Mousse
- Chia Seed Pudding
- Banana Bread (Low-Sugar)
- Greek Yogurt Parfait with Berries
- Almond Butter Brownies
- Coconut Macaroons
- Apple Cinnamon Baked Chips
- Vegan Chocolate Fudge
- Baked Pears with Cinnamon
- Raw Energy Bites
- Oatmeal Raisin Cookies (Sugar-Free)
- Chocolate-Covered Almonds
- Sweet Potato Brownies
- Almond Joy Energy Bars
- Frozen Yogurt Bark with Fruit
- Carrot Cake Energy Bites
- Fruit Sorbet
- Coconut Milk Rice Pudding
- Raw Chocolate Coconut Balls
- Healthy Banana Ice Cream
- Protein-Packed Chocolate Chip Cookies
- Chia Jam
- Healthy Cheesecake (Made with Greek Yogurt)
- Apple Nachos with Almond Butter
- Cinnamon Coconut Energy Balls
- Almond Flour Chocolate Chip Cookies
- Chocolate-Dipped Frozen Bananas
- Peach and Coconut Crumble
- Zucchini Bread (Low-Sugar)
- Dark Chocolate Avocado Truffles
- Coconut Yogurt with Fresh Berries
- Acai Bowl
- Strawberry Chia Jam
- Vegan Chocolate Mousse
- Oatmeal Date Balls

- Roasted Cinnamon Apples
- Chocolate-Covered Frozen Strawberries
- Coconut-Cashew Truffles
- Frozen Fruit Popsicles
- Raw Vegan Chocolate Cake
- Greek Yogurt with Honey and Walnuts
- Baked Banana Fries
- Chia Pudding with Almond Milk
- Mixed Berry Compote
- Cashew Cream Pie
- Banana Oat Cookies
- Raw Blueberry Cheesecake
- No-Bake Peanut Butter Bars
- Mango Sorbet
- Frozen Chocolate-Covered Almonds

Avocado Chocolate Mousse

Ingredients:

- 2 ripe avocados, peeled and pitted
- 1/4 cup unsweetened cocoa powder
- 1/4 cup maple syrup or honey
- 1/2 teaspoon vanilla extract
- Pinch of salt
- 1/4 cup almond milk (or any milk of choice)

Instructions:

1. In a blender or food processor, combine avocados, cocoa powder, maple syrup, vanilla extract, and salt.
2. Blend until smooth and creamy, adding almond milk a little at a time to reach desired consistency.
3. Chill in the fridge for at least 30 minutes before serving.
4. Serve with berries or whipped cream, if desired.

Chia Seed Pudding

Ingredients:

- 1/2 cup chia seeds
- 2 cups unsweetened almond milk (or any milk of choice)
- 2 tablespoons maple syrup or honey
- 1 teaspoon vanilla extract

Instructions:

1. In a bowl or jar, combine chia seeds, almond milk, maple syrup, and vanilla extract.
2. Stir well to ensure the chia seeds are evenly distributed.
3. Cover and refrigerate for at least 4 hours or overnight to allow the chia seeds to absorb the liquid and thicken.
4. Serve with fresh fruit, nuts, or granola.

Banana Bread (Low-Sugar)

Ingredients:

- 2 ripe bananas, mashed
- 1/4 cup unsweetened applesauce
- 1/4 cup honey or maple syrup
- 1 large egg
- 1 teaspoon vanilla extract
- 1 1/2 cups whole wheat flour
- 1 teaspoon baking powder
- 1/2 teaspoon baking soda
- 1/2 teaspoon ground cinnamon
- 1/4 teaspoon salt

Instructions:

1. Preheat the oven to 350°F (175°C). Grease or line a loaf pan with parchment paper.
2. In a large bowl, mix mashed bananas, applesauce, honey (or maple syrup), egg, and vanilla extract.
3. In a separate bowl, whisk together whole wheat flour, baking powder, baking soda, cinnamon, and salt.
4. Gradually add the dry ingredients to the wet ingredients, stirring until just combined.
5. Pour the batter into the prepared loaf pan and bake for 45-55 minutes, or until a toothpick comes out clean.
6. Let cool before slicing.

Greek Yogurt Parfait with Berries

Ingredients:

- 2 cups plain Greek yogurt
- 2 tablespoons honey or maple syrup
- 1 teaspoon vanilla extract
- 1 cup mixed berries (blueberries, strawberries, raspberries)
- 1/4 cup granola (optional)

Instructions:

1. In a bowl, mix Greek yogurt with honey and vanilla extract.
2. Layer the yogurt mixture with fresh berries in serving glasses or bowls.
3. Top with granola if desired for added crunch.
4. Serve immediately or chill for a few hours.

Almond Butter Brownies

Ingredients:

- 1/2 cup almond butter
- 2 large eggs
- 1/2 cup coconut sugar (or maple syrup)
- 1/4 cup unsweetened cocoa powder
- 1/2 teaspoon vanilla extract
- 1/4 teaspoon baking soda
- Pinch of salt

Instructions:

1. Preheat the oven to 350°F (175°C). Grease or line a baking dish with parchment paper.
2. In a large bowl, whisk together almond butter, eggs, coconut sugar, cocoa powder, vanilla extract, baking soda, and salt.
3. Pour the batter into the prepared baking dish and spread evenly.
4. Bake for 15-20 minutes, or until a toothpick inserted comes out clean.
5. Let cool before slicing into squares.

Coconut Macaroons

Ingredients:

- 2 cups unsweetened shredded coconut
- 1/4 cup honey or maple syrup
- 2 large egg whites
- 1 teaspoon vanilla extract
- Pinch of salt

Instructions:

1. Preheat the oven to 325°F (165°C). Line a baking sheet with parchment paper.
2. In a bowl, mix shredded coconut, honey (or maple syrup), egg whites, vanilla extract, and salt until combined.
3. Scoop spoonfuls of the mixture and form small mounds on the baking sheet.
4. Bake for 10-12 minutes until golden brown. Let cool before serving.

Apple Cinnamon Baked Chips

Ingredients:

- 2 apples, thinly sliced
- 1 teaspoon ground cinnamon
- 1 tablespoon coconut sugar (optional)

Instructions:

1. Preheat the oven to 225°F (107°C). Line a baking sheet with parchment paper.
2. Arrange the apple slices in a single layer on the baking sheet.
3. Sprinkle with cinnamon and coconut sugar, if using.
4. Bake for 1 1/2 to 2 hours, flipping halfway through, until the apples are crisp and golden.
5. Let cool before serving.

Vegan Chocolate Fudge

Ingredients:

- 1 1/2 cups dark chocolate chips (dairy-free)
- 1/2 cup coconut milk (full-fat)
- 1/4 cup maple syrup
- 1/2 teaspoon vanilla extract
- 1/4 cup chopped nuts (optional)

Instructions:

1. In a saucepan, heat coconut milk and maple syrup over low heat until warm.
2. Stir in chocolate chips until melted and smooth.
3. Remove from heat and stir in vanilla extract.
4. Pour the mixture into a lined baking dish and spread evenly.
5. Top with chopped nuts, if desired, and refrigerate for at least 2 hours to set.
6. Cut into squares and serve.

Baked Pears with Cinnamon

Ingredients:

- 4 pears, halved and cored
- 1/4 cup honey or maple syrup
- 1 teaspoon ground cinnamon
- 1 tablespoon lemon juice

Instructions:

1. Preheat the oven to 350°F (175°C). Place pear halves in a baking dish.
2. Drizzle with honey (or maple syrup) and sprinkle with cinnamon.
3. Add a few drops of lemon juice to each pear half.
4. Bake for 25-30 minutes until the pears are tender and caramelized.
5. Serve warm with a dollop of yogurt or whipped cream, if desired.

Raw Energy Bites

Ingredients:

- 1 cup rolled oats
- 1/2 cup nut butter (almond, peanut, etc.)
- 1/4 cup honey or maple syrup
- 1/4 cup ground flaxseed
- 1/4 cup chocolate chips or dried fruit (optional)
- 1 teaspoon vanilla extract
- Pinch of salt

Instructions:

1. In a bowl, combine oats, nut butter, honey (or maple syrup), flaxseed, and vanilla extract. Stir until well combined.
2. Add chocolate chips or dried fruit, if desired.
3. Roll the mixture into 1-inch balls and place on a parchment-lined baking sheet.
4. Refrigerate for at least 1 hour to firm up before serving.

Oatmeal Raisin Cookies (Sugar-Free)

Ingredients:

- 2 cups rolled oats
- 1/2 cup unsweetened applesauce
- 1/4 cup almond butter or peanut butter
- 1/4 cup raisins
- 1 teaspoon cinnamon
- 1/4 teaspoon salt
- 1/2 teaspoon vanilla extract
- 1 egg

Instructions:

1. Preheat the oven to 350°F (175°C) and line a baking sheet with parchment paper.
2. In a bowl, mix together oats, applesauce, almond butter, raisins, cinnamon, salt, vanilla extract, and egg.
3. Drop spoonfuls of dough onto the baking sheet and flatten slightly with the back of the spoon.
4. Bake for 12-15 minutes until golden and firm. Let cool before serving.

Chocolate-Covered Almonds

Ingredients:

- 1 cup raw almonds
- 1 cup dark chocolate chips (dairy-free)
- 1 tablespoon coconut oil

Instructions:

1. Preheat the oven to 350°F (175°C) and toast the almonds on a baking sheet for 8-10 minutes.
2. In a microwave-safe bowl, melt the dark chocolate chips and coconut oil together in 30-second intervals, stirring until smooth.
3. Dip each almond into the melted chocolate and place it back on the parchment-lined baking sheet.
4. Refrigerate for 30 minutes to allow the chocolate to set.

Sweet Potato Brownies

Ingredients:

- 1 medium sweet potato, cooked and mashed
- 1/2 cup unsweetened cocoa powder
- 1/4 cup almond flour
- 1/4 cup maple syrup
- 1/4 cup almond butter
- 1 teaspoon vanilla extract
- 1/2 teaspoon baking powder
- Pinch of salt

Instructions:

1. Preheat the oven to 350°F (175°C) and grease a baking pan.
2. In a bowl, combine mashed sweet potato, cocoa powder, almond flour, maple syrup, almond butter, vanilla extract, baking powder, and salt.
3. Mix until smooth and pour into the prepared pan.
4. Bake for 20-25 minutes until firm. Let cool before slicing into squares.

Almond Joy Energy Bars

Ingredients:

- 1 cup oats
- 1/2 cup unsweetened shredded coconut
- 1/2 cup almond butter
- 1/4 cup maple syrup or honey
- 1/2 cup dark chocolate chips
- 1/4 cup chopped almonds

Instructions:

1. In a bowl, combine oats, shredded coconut, almond butter, maple syrup (or honey), and dark chocolate chips. Mix well.
2. Press the mixture into a greased or lined baking dish and top with chopped almonds.
3. Refrigerate for at least 2 hours to set. Cut into bars before serving.

Frozen Yogurt Bark with Fruit

Ingredients:

- 2 cups plain Greek yogurt
- 1-2 tablespoons honey or maple syrup (optional)
- 1/2 cup fresh mixed berries (strawberries, blueberries, raspberries)
- 1/4 cup unsweetened shredded coconut (optional)

Instructions:

1. Line a baking sheet with parchment paper.
2. In a bowl, mix Greek yogurt with honey or maple syrup if desired.
3. Spread the yogurt mixture evenly over the baking sheet.
4. Top with mixed berries and shredded coconut.
5. Freeze for 2-3 hours, or until solid. Break into pieces and serve.

Carrot Cake Energy Bites

Ingredients:

- 1 cup rolled oats
- 1/2 cup grated carrots
- 1/4 cup almond butter
- 1 tablespoon honey or maple syrup
- 1 teaspoon cinnamon
- 1/4 teaspoon ground ginger
- 1/4 cup chopped walnuts (optional)

Instructions:

1. In a bowl, combine oats, grated carrots, almond butter, honey (or maple syrup), cinnamon, and ginger.
2. Mix until well combined. Add walnuts if desired.
3. Roll the mixture into 1-inch balls and refrigerate for 30 minutes to set.
4. Serve chilled or at room temperature.

Fruit Sorbet

Ingredients:

- 2 cups fresh fruit (mango, berries, or peaches)
- 2 tablespoons honey or maple syrup (optional)
- 1 tablespoon lemon juice

Instructions:

1. In a blender, combine fruit, honey (or maple syrup), and lemon juice. Blend until smooth.
2. Pour the mixture into a shallow dish and freeze for 2-3 hours.
3. Scrape with a fork every 30 minutes to break up the ice crystals and create a fluffy texture.
4. Serve once fully frozen.

Coconut Milk Rice Pudding

Ingredients:

- 1/2 cup Arborio rice
- 2 cups coconut milk
- 1/2 cup water
- 1/4 cup maple syrup or honey
- 1/2 teaspoon vanilla extract
- 1/4 teaspoon ground cinnamon
- Pinch of salt

Instructions:

1. In a saucepan, combine Arborio rice, coconut milk, water, maple syrup (or honey), vanilla extract, cinnamon, and salt.
2. Cook over medium heat, stirring frequently, for 20-25 minutes, until the rice is tender and the mixture thickens.
3. Let cool slightly before serving. Garnish with extra cinnamon or coconut flakes if desired.

Raw Chocolate Coconut Balls

Ingredients:

- 1 cup unsweetened shredded coconut
- 1/2 cup raw cacao powder
- 2 tablespoons maple syrup or honey
- 2 tablespoons coconut oil, melted
- 1 teaspoon vanilla extract
- Pinch of salt

Instructions:

1. In a bowl, combine shredded coconut, cacao powder, maple syrup (or honey), coconut oil, vanilla extract, and salt.
2. Mix until the dough is sticky. Roll into 1-inch balls.
3. Place on a parchment-lined baking sheet and refrigerate for 1 hour to set.
4. Serve chilled.

Healthy Banana Ice Cream

Ingredients:

- 2 ripe bananas, sliced and frozen
- 1/2 teaspoon vanilla extract
- 2 tablespoons almond milk (or any milk of choice)

Instructions:

1. Place the frozen banana slices in a blender or food processor.
2. Add vanilla extract and almond milk.
3. Blend until smooth and creamy, scraping down the sides as needed.
4. Serve immediately as soft-serve or freeze for 1-2 hours for a firmer consistency.

Protein-Packed Chocolate Chip Cookies

Ingredients:

- 1 1/2 cups rolled oats
- 1/2 cup almond flour
- 1/4 cup protein powder (vanilla or chocolate flavor)
- 1/2 teaspoon baking soda
- 1/4 teaspoon salt
- 1/4 cup unsweetened almond butter
- 1/4 cup honey or maple syrup
- 1 large egg
- 1 teaspoon vanilla extract
- 1/2 cup dark chocolate chips

Instructions:

1. Preheat the oven to 350°F (175°C) and line a baking sheet with parchment paper.
2. In a bowl, combine oats, almond flour, protein powder, baking soda, and salt.
3. In another bowl, mix almond butter, honey, egg, and vanilla extract.
4. Add the wet ingredients to the dry ingredients and stir until combined. Fold in chocolate chips.
5. Drop spoonfuls of dough onto the baking sheet and flatten slightly.
6. Bake for 10-12 minutes until golden. Let cool before serving.

Chia Jam

Ingredients:

- 2 cups fresh or frozen fruit (berries, peaches, etc.)
- 1 tablespoon lemon juice
- 2 tablespoons maple syrup or honey (optional)
- 2 tablespoons chia seeds

Instructions:

1. In a saucepan, heat the fruit and lemon juice over medium heat, mashing the fruit with a fork or potato masher.
2. Stir in maple syrup or honey if using. Cook for 5-7 minutes until the fruit softens.
3. Remove from heat and stir in chia seeds. Let the mixture cool to thicken.
4. Transfer to a jar and refrigerate for up to 2 weeks. Use as a spread or topping.

Healthy Cheesecake (Made with Greek Yogurt)

Ingredients:

- 2 cups plain Greek yogurt
- 1/2 cup cream cheese, softened
- 1/4 cup honey or maple syrup
- 1 teaspoon vanilla extract
- 1/4 cup coconut flour (or any flour of choice)
- 1/4 cup almond meal (optional, for crust)

Instructions:

1. Preheat the oven to 350°F (175°C) and grease a small pie or tart pan.
2. In a bowl, combine Greek yogurt, cream cheese, honey (or maple syrup), and vanilla extract until smooth.
3. Add coconut flour and mix until well combined. Pour the filling into the prepared pan.
4. Bake for 20-25 minutes until set in the middle.
5. Let cool to room temperature before refrigerating for 2 hours. Serve chilled.

Apple Nachos with Almond Butter

Ingredients:

- 2 apples, thinly sliced
- 1/4 cup almond butter
- 2 tablespoons honey
- 1/4 cup granola
- 1 tablespoon chia seeds (optional)

Instructions:

1. Arrange the apple slices on a serving plate, slightly overlapping.
2. In a small bowl, warm almond butter and honey together in the microwave for 15-20 seconds, then stir until smooth.
3. Drizzle the almond butter mixture over the apple slices.
4. Top with granola and chia seeds (if using). Serve immediately.

Cinnamon Coconut Energy Balls

Ingredients:

- 1 cup unsweetened shredded coconut
- 1/2 cup rolled oats
- 1/4 cup almond butter
- 1 tablespoon honey or maple syrup
- 1/2 teaspoon ground cinnamon
- Pinch of salt

Instructions:

1. In a bowl, combine shredded coconut, oats, almond butter, honey, cinnamon, and salt.
2. Mix until everything is well combined.
3. Roll the mixture into 1-inch balls and refrigerate for 30 minutes to set.
4. Store in the fridge for up to 1 week.

Almond Flour Chocolate Chip Cookies

Ingredients:

- 2 cups almond flour
- 1/2 teaspoon baking soda
- 1/4 teaspoon salt
- 1/4 cup coconut oil, melted
- 1/4 cup maple syrup or honey
- 1 large egg
- 1 teaspoon vanilla extract
- 1/2 cup dark chocolate chips

Instructions:

1. Preheat the oven to 350°F (175°C) and line a baking sheet with parchment paper.
2. In a bowl, mix almond flour, baking soda, and salt.
3. In another bowl, combine coconut oil, maple syrup, egg, and vanilla extract.
4. Add the wet ingredients to the dry ingredients and mix until combined. Fold in chocolate chips.
5. Drop spoonfuls of dough onto the baking sheet and bake for 10-12 minutes. Let cool before serving.

Chocolate-Dipped Frozen Bananas

Ingredients:

- 2 ripe bananas, sliced into 1-inch rounds
- 1 cup dark chocolate chips
- 1 tablespoon coconut oil
- 1/4 cup chopped nuts or shredded coconut (optional)

Instructions:

1. Place banana slices on a parchment-lined baking sheet and freeze for 1-2 hours.
2. In a microwave-safe bowl, melt dark chocolate chips and coconut oil in 30-second intervals, stirring until smooth.
3. Dip each frozen banana slice in the melted chocolate and place back on the baking sheet.
4. Top with chopped nuts or shredded coconut if desired.
5. Freeze again for 1 hour until the chocolate hardens. Serve immediately.

Peach and Coconut Crumble

Ingredients for Filling:

- 4 ripe peaches, peeled and chopped
- 1 tablespoon lemon juice
- 1/4 cup maple syrup
- 1/2 teaspoon ground cinnamon

For Topping:

- 1 cup unsweetened shredded coconut
- 1/4 cup almond flour
- 1 tablespoon coconut oil, melted
- 1/4 cup oats
- 1 tablespoon maple syrup

Instructions:

1. Preheat the oven to 350°F (175°C).
2. In a bowl, mix chopped peaches, lemon juice, maple syrup, and cinnamon. Place in a baking dish.
3. In another bowl, mix shredded coconut, almond flour, coconut oil, oats, and maple syrup until crumbly.
4. Sprinkle the topping evenly over the peach mixture.
5. Bake for 25-30 minutes, until the topping is golden brown and the filling is bubbly. Let cool slightly before serving.

Zucchini Bread (Low-Sugar)

Ingredients:

- 2 cups all-purpose flour
- 1 teaspoon baking powder
- 1/2 teaspoon baking soda
- 1/2 teaspoon ground cinnamon
- 1/4 teaspoon salt
- 2 medium zucchinis, grated
- 2 large eggs
- 1/4 cup coconut oil, melted
- 1/4 cup unsweetened applesauce
- 1/2 cup stevia or monk fruit sweetener

Instructions:

1. Preheat the oven to 350°F (175°C) and grease a loaf pan.
2. In a bowl, combine flour, baking powder, baking soda, cinnamon, and salt.
3. In a separate bowl, whisk together eggs, coconut oil, applesauce, and sweetener.
4. Stir the dry ingredients into the wet mixture. Fold in grated zucchini.
5. Pour the batter into the prepared pan and bake for 45-50 minutes, or until a toothpick comes out clean. Let cool before serving.

Dark Chocolate Avocado Truffles

Ingredients:

- 1 ripe avocado, mashed
- 1 cup dark chocolate chips
- 1 teaspoon vanilla extract
- 1/4 cup cocoa powder (optional)

Instructions:

1. In a microwave-safe bowl, melt dark chocolate chips in 30-second intervals, stirring until smooth.
2. Stir in mashed avocado and vanilla extract until fully combined.
3. Refrigerate for 1-2 hours until the mixture is firm enough to roll into balls.
4. Roll into 1-inch balls and coat in cocoa powder, if desired.
5. Store in the fridge for up to 1 week.

Coconut Yogurt with Fresh Berries

Ingredients:

- 1 cup unsweetened coconut yogurt
- 1/2 cup fresh mixed berries (strawberries, blueberries, raspberries)
- 1 tablespoon honey or maple syrup (optional)
- 1 tablespoon chia seeds (optional)

Instructions:

1. Spoon the coconut yogurt into a bowl.
2. Top with fresh berries and drizzle with honey or maple syrup.
3. Sprinkle with chia seeds for extra nutrition. Serve immediately.

Acai Bowl

Ingredients:

- 1 packet frozen acai puree
- 1/2 cup unsweetened almond milk (or any milk of choice)
- 1/2 banana
- 1/4 cup granola
- 1/4 cup fresh fruit (berries, kiwi, etc.)
- 1 tablespoon coconut flakes

Instructions:

1. Blend the frozen acai puree, almond milk, and banana until smooth.
2. Pour the acai mixture into a bowl and top with granola, fresh fruit, and coconut flakes.
3. Serve immediately.

Strawberry Chia Jam

Ingredients:

- 2 cups fresh strawberries, chopped
- 2 tablespoons chia seeds
- 2 tablespoons honey or maple syrup
- 1 tablespoon lemon juice

Instructions:

1. In a saucepan, cook strawberries and honey (or maple syrup) over medium heat, stirring occasionally for 5-7 minutes.
2. Mash the strawberries with a fork or potato masher as they cook.
3. Stir in chia seeds and lemon juice. Continue to cook for another 3-5 minutes until thickened.
4. Remove from heat and let cool. Transfer to a jar and refrigerate for up to 1 week.

Vegan Chocolate Mousse

Ingredients:

- 2 ripe avocados, peeled and pitted
- 1/4 cup unsweetened cocoa powder
- 1/4 cup maple syrup or agave nectar
- 1/2 teaspoon vanilla extract
- Pinch of salt
- 1/4 cup almond milk (or any plant-based milk)

Instructions:

1. In a blender or food processor, combine avocados, cocoa powder, maple syrup, vanilla extract, and salt.
2. Blend until smooth and creamy. Add almond milk a little at a time to reach desired consistency.
3. Refrigerate for at least 30 minutes before serving.
4. Serve chilled with fresh berries or whipped coconut cream.

Oatmeal Date Balls

Ingredients:

- 1 1/2 cups rolled oats
- 1/2 cup pitted dates, chopped
- 1/4 cup almond butter
- 2 tablespoons chia seeds
- 1 tablespoon maple syrup
- 1/4 teaspoon cinnamon
- 1/4 teaspoon vanilla extract

Instructions:

1. In a food processor, combine oats, chopped dates, almond butter, chia seeds, maple syrup, cinnamon, and vanilla extract.
2. Pulse until the mixture sticks together when pressed.
3. Roll the mixture into 1-inch balls and refrigerate for at least 30 minutes to set.
4. Store in an airtight container in the fridge.

Roasted Cinnamon Apples

Ingredients:

- 4 apples, peeled, cored, and sliced
- 1 tablespoon maple syrup or honey
- 1 teaspoon ground cinnamon
- 1/4 teaspoon ground nutmeg
- 1 tablespoon lemon juice

Instructions:

1. Preheat the oven to 350°F (175°C) and line a baking sheet with parchment paper.
2. In a bowl, toss apple slices with maple syrup (or honey), cinnamon, nutmeg, and lemon juice.
3. Spread the apples evenly on the baking sheet.
4. Roast for 25-30 minutes, stirring halfway through, until the apples are tender and golden.
5. Serve warm with a sprinkle of cinnamon or a dollop of yogurt.

Chocolate-Covered Frozen Strawberries

Ingredients:

- 1 pint fresh strawberries, washed and dried
- 1 cup dark chocolate chips (dairy-free)
- 1 tablespoon coconut oil (optional)

Instructions:

1. Line a baking sheet with parchment paper.
2. Melt the chocolate chips with coconut oil (if using) in a microwave-safe bowl, stirring every 30 seconds until smooth.
3. Dip each strawberry into the melted chocolate, covering it completely.
4. Place the chocolate-covered strawberries on the baking sheet and freeze for at least 1 hour until the chocolate hardens.
5. Serve chilled or frozen.

Coconut-Cashew Truffles

Ingredients:

- 1/2 cup cashews
- 1/2 cup shredded unsweetened coconut
- 1 tablespoon maple syrup
- 1/2 teaspoon vanilla extract
- Pinch of salt
- 1/4 cup melted dark chocolate (optional, for coating)

Instructions:

1. In a food processor, blend cashews and shredded coconut until finely ground.
2. Add maple syrup, vanilla extract, and salt, and blend until the mixture sticks together.
3. Roll the mixture into small balls and refrigerate for 30 minutes to set.
4. If desired, dip the truffles in melted dark chocolate and refrigerate again until set.

Frozen Fruit Popsicles

Ingredients:

- 2 cups mixed fresh fruit (berries, mango, banana, etc.)
- 1/2 cup coconut water or almond milk
- 1 tablespoon honey or maple syrup (optional)

Instructions:

1. In a blender, blend mixed fruit with coconut water (or almond milk) and honey (if using).
2. Pour the mixture into popsicle molds and insert sticks.
3. Freeze for at least 4 hours or until fully frozen.
4. To release, run warm water over the outside of the molds.

Raw Vegan Chocolate Cake

Ingredients for Cake:

- 1 1/2 cups almonds
- 1/2 cup unsweetened cocoa powder
- 1/4 cup pitted dates
- 2 tablespoons maple syrup
- 1/4 teaspoon vanilla extract
- Pinch of salt

For Frosting:

- 1/2 cup raw cashews, soaked overnight
- 1/4 cup coconut oil, melted
- 1/4 cup maple syrup
- 2 tablespoons unsweetened cocoa powder

Instructions:

1. For the cake, process almonds, cocoa powder, dates, maple syrup, vanilla extract, and salt in a food processor until a dough-like consistency forms.
2. Press the mixture into the bottom of a small cake pan lined with parchment paper.
3. For the frosting, blend soaked cashews, coconut oil, maple syrup, and cocoa powder in a blender until smooth.
4. Spread the frosting over the cake and refrigerate for 1-2 hours before serving.

Greek Yogurt with Honey and Walnuts

Ingredients:

- 1 cup plain Greek yogurt
- 1 tablespoon honey
- 1/4 cup chopped walnuts

Instructions:

1. Spoon Greek yogurt into a bowl.
2. Drizzle with honey and sprinkle with chopped walnuts.
3. Serve immediately or refrigerate for later.

Baked Banana Fries

Ingredients:

- 2 ripe bananas, peeled and cut into thin fries
- 1 tablespoon coconut oil, melted
- 1/2 teaspoon cinnamon
- Pinch of salt

Instructions:

1. Preheat the oven to 375°F (190°C) and line a baking sheet with parchment paper.
2. Toss the banana fries in melted coconut oil, cinnamon, and salt.
3. Arrange them in a single layer on the baking sheet.
4. Bake for 15-20 minutes, flipping halfway through, until golden and crispy on the edges.
5. Serve warm.

Chia Pudding with Almond Milk

Ingredients:

- 1/4 cup chia seeds
- 1 cup almond milk (or any plant-based milk)
- 1 tablespoon maple syrup (optional)
- 1/2 teaspoon vanilla extract

Instructions:

1. In a bowl or jar, combine chia seeds, almond milk, maple syrup, and vanilla extract.
2. Stir well and refrigerate for at least 4 hours or overnight to thicken.
3. Serve with fresh fruit or granola on top.

Mixed Berry Compote

Ingredients:

- 2 cups mixed berries (strawberries, raspberries, blueberries, etc.)
- 2 tablespoons maple syrup or honey
- 1 tablespoon lemon juice

Instructions:

1. In a saucepan, combine mixed berries, maple syrup (or honey), and lemon juice.
2. Cook over medium heat for 5-7 minutes, mashing the berries with a spoon as they cook.
3. Reduce the heat and simmer for another 5 minutes until thickened.
4. Let cool before serving over yogurt, pancakes, or waffles.

Cashew Cream Pie

Ingredients:

- 1 1/2 cups raw cashews, soaked for 4 hours or overnight
- 1/4 cup coconut oil, melted
- 1/4 cup maple syrup
- 1/4 cup fresh lemon juice
- 1 teaspoon vanilla extract
- 1/2 cup unsweetened coconut milk (or any plant-based milk)
- 1 pre-made pie crust (graham cracker or nut-based)

Instructions:

1. Drain and rinse the soaked cashews. In a blender or food processor, combine cashews, coconut oil, maple syrup, lemon juice, vanilla extract, and coconut milk. Blend until smooth and creamy.
2. Pour the cashew mixture into the pre-made pie crust.
3. Refrigerate for at least 4 hours or overnight to allow the filling to set.
4. Serve chilled with fresh fruit or coconut flakes on top, if desired.

Banana Oat Cookies

Ingredients:

- 2 ripe bananas, mashed
- 1 cup rolled oats
- 1/2 teaspoon cinnamon
- 1/4 cup raisins or chocolate chips (optional)
- 1/4 cup chopped nuts (optional)

Instructions:

1. Preheat the oven to 350°F (175°C) and line a baking sheet with parchment paper.
2. In a bowl, mix together mashed bananas, oats, cinnamon, and any optional add-ins.
3. Drop spoonfuls of dough onto the baking sheet and flatten slightly.
4. Bake for 10-12 minutes until golden. Let cool before serving.

Raw Blueberry Cheesecake

Ingredients for Crust:

- 1 1/2 cups almonds or walnuts
- 1/2 cup pitted dates
- 2 tablespoons coconut oil, melted

For Filling:

- 2 cups raw cashews, soaked for 4 hours or overnight
- 1/2 cup fresh or frozen blueberries
- 1/4 cup maple syrup
- 1/4 cup lemon juice
- 1 teaspoon vanilla extract
- 1/4 cup coconut oil, melted

Instructions:

1. For the crust: In a food processor, blend almonds (or walnuts) and dates until the mixture sticks together. Add melted coconut oil and pulse to combine.
2. Press the crust mixture into the bottom of a greased springform pan.
3. For the filling: In a blender, combine soaked cashews, blueberries, maple syrup, lemon juice, vanilla extract, and melted coconut oil. Blend until smooth.
4. Pour the blueberry filling onto the crust and smooth the top.
5. Refrigerate for at least 4 hours or overnight to set. Serve chilled.

No-Bake Peanut Butter Bars

Ingredients:

- 1 cup peanut butter (smooth or chunky)
- 1/4 cup honey or maple syrup
- 1 1/2 cups rolled oats
- 1/4 cup unsweetened cocoa powder
- 1 teaspoon vanilla extract
- 1/4 teaspoon salt
- 1/4 cup dark chocolate chips (optional, for topping)

Instructions:

1. In a bowl, combine peanut butter, honey (or maple syrup), oats, cocoa powder, vanilla extract, and salt. Stir until fully combined.
2. Press the mixture into a greased or parchment-lined 8x8-inch baking dish.
3. If desired, melt dark chocolate chips and drizzle over the top of the bars.
4. Refrigerate for 2-3 hours until firm. Cut into squares and serve.

Mango Sorbet

Ingredients:

- 3 ripe mangoes, peeled and chopped
- 1/4 cup lime juice
- 1 tablespoon honey or maple syrup (optional)

Instructions:

1. In a blender or food processor, blend chopped mangoes, lime juice, and honey (if using) until smooth.
2. Pour the mixture into a shallow dish and freeze for 2-3 hours.
3. Scrape with a fork every 30 minutes to break up the ice crystals and create a fluffy texture.
4. Serve once fully frozen.

Frozen Chocolate-Covered Almonds

Ingredients:

- 1 cup raw almonds
- 1 cup dark chocolate chips (dairy-free)
- 1 tablespoon coconut oil

Instructions:

1. Preheat the oven to 350°F (175°C) and toast the almonds on a baking sheet for 8-10 minutes.
2. In a microwave-safe bowl, melt the dark chocolate chips and coconut oil in 30-second intervals, stirring until smooth.
3. Dip each toasted almond into the melted chocolate and place back on the parchment-lined baking sheet.
4. Freeze for at least 30 minutes until the chocolate hardens.
5. Serve chilled.

www.ingramcontent.com/pod-product-compliance
Lightning Source LLC
LaVergne TN
LVHW061955070526
838199LV00060B/4126